Circus

Circus Animal Acts

Denise M. Jordan

Heinemann Library
Chicago, Illinois

Customer Service 888-454-2279
Visit our website at www.heinemannlibrary.com

Designed by Sue Emerson, Heinemann Library
Printed and bound in the U.S.A. by Lake Book

06 05 04 03 02
10 9 8 7 6 5 4 3 2 1

Library of Congress Cataloging-in-Publication Data
Jordan, Denise M.
    Circus animal acts / Denise Jordan.
        p. cm. — (Circus)
Includes index.
Summary: Introduces circus animals, how they are trained, and the types of tricks different animals can perform.
    ISBN: 1-58810-543-1 (HC), 1-58810-751-5 (Pbk.)
    1. Circus animals—Juvenile literature. [1. Circus animals.] I. Title.
    GV1829 .J67 2002
    791.3'2—dc21

                            2001004791

Acknowledgments
The author and publishers are grateful to the following for permission to reproduce copyright material:
p. 4 National Geographic Society; p. 5 B. Seed/Trip; pp. 6, 21 S. Grant/Trip; p. 7 Nik Wheeler/Corbis; pp. 8, 10, 22 Robert Frerck/Odyssey/Chicago; p. 9 Eric Smith/Trip; pp. 11, 16 Greg Williams/Heinemann Library; p. 12 Red Saunders/Trip; p. 13 R. Osf Cannon/Animals Animals; p. 14 ChromoSohm/Sohm/Unicorn Stock Photos; p. 15 Gerald Lin/Unicorn Stock Photos; p. 17 Tom & Dee Ann McCarthy/Unicorn Stock Photos; p. 18 Dean Conger/Corbis; p. 19 Marshall Prescott/Unicorn Stock Photos; p. 20 Eugene G. Schulz

Cover photograph courtesy of Rafael Crisostomo

Every effort has been made to contact copyright holders of any material reproduced in this book. Any omissions will be rectified in subsequent printings if notice is given to the publisher.

Special thanks to our advisory panel for their help in the preparation of this book:
Eileen Day, Preschool Teacher
Chicago, IL

Paula Fischer, K–1 Teacher
Indianapolis, IN

Sandra Gilbert,
Library Media Specialist
Houston, TX

Angela Leeper,
Educational Consultant
North Carolina Department
of Public Instruction
Raleigh, NC

Pam McDonald, Reading Teacher
Winter Springs, FL

Melinda Murphy,
Library Media Specialist
Houston, TX

Helen Rosenberg, MLS
Chicago, IL

Anna Marie Varakin,
Reading Instructor
Western Maryland College

The publishers would also like to thank Fred Dahlinger, Jr., Director of Collections and Research at the Circus World Museum in Baraboo, Wisconsin, and Smita Parida for their help in reviewing the contents of this book.

Some words are shown in bold, **like this**.
You can find them in the picture glossary on page 23.

Contents

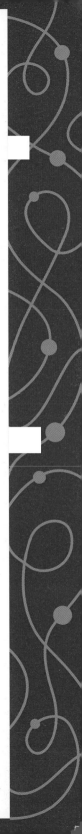

What Are Circus Animals?

Circus animals do tricks.

Some circus animal acts are exciting.

Some circus animals are like pets.

All circus animals are trained.

How Do Circus Animals Learn Tricks?

Animal trainers teach circus animals to do tricks.

They take good care of the animals.

They give the animals treats.

The animals do the trick over and over.

When Does Circus Training Begin?

Some animals are born in the circus.

They learn tricks when they are babies.

Older animals can learn tricks, too.

What Kinds of Animals Are in the Circus?

tiger

lion

There are lions and tigers in the circus.

There are elephants.

There are other kinds of animals, too.

What Can Sea Lions Do?

Sea lions can climb stairs.

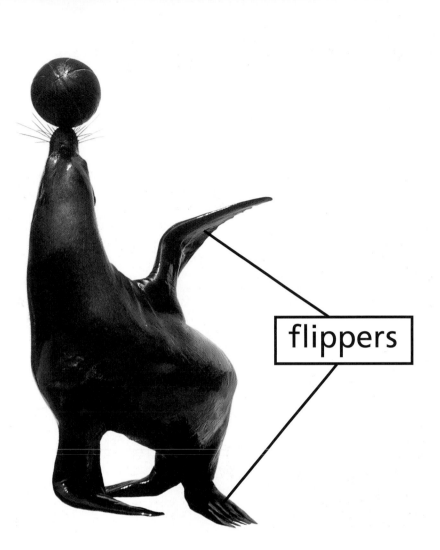

flippers

They can balance things on their noses.

They can clap with their **flippers**.

What Can Lions and Tigers Do?

Lions and tigers move very fast.

They snarl and roar.

Lions and tigers can jump through hoops of fire.

They are very large animals.

What Can Elephants Do?

Elephants can stand on their back legs.

They can lift people high in the air.

trunk

Elephants are very strong.

They have long **trunks**.

What Can Horses Do?

Some horses can learn tricks.

These horses can dance.

Riders can do tricks on the
horses' backs.

Where Do Circus Animals Live?

Circus animals live in **cages**.

This cage is a wagon, too.

trailer

Circus animals ride around in **trailers**.

When the circus is closed, they live on a farm.

Quiz

What are these circus things?

Can you find them in the book?

Look for the answers on page 24.

? ? ?

Picture Glossary

animal trainer
page 6

trailer
page 21

cage
page 20

trunk
page 17

flipper
page 13

Note to Parents and Teachers

Reading for information is an important part of a child's literacy development. Learning begins with a question about something. Help children think of themselves as investigators and researchers by encouraging their questions about the world around them. Each chapter in this book begins with a question. Read the question together. Look at the pictures. Talk about what you think the answer might be. Then read the text to find out if your predictions were correct. Think of other questions you could ask about the topic, and discuss where you might find the answers. Assist children in using the picture glossary and the index to practice new vocabulary and research skills.

Index

Answers to quiz on page 22

tiger | lion | animal trainer